Hayley Westenra

ODYSSEY

WISE PUBLICATIONS
part of The Music Sales Group
London / New York / Paris / Sydney / Copenhagen / Berlin / Madrid / Tokyo

Exclusive distributors:

Music Sales Limited
8/9 Frith Street, London, W1D 3JB, England.

Music Sales Pty Limited
120 Rothschild Avenue, Rosebery, NSW 2018, Australia.

Order No. AM984599
ISBN 1-84609-324-4
This book © Copyright 2005 by Wise Publications,
a division of Music Sales Limited.

Edited by Ann Farmer.
Music arrangements by Derek Jones.
Music processed by Paul Ewers Music Design.

Printed in the United Kingdom by
Caligraving Limited, Thetford, Norfolk.

www.musicsales.com

Your Guarantee of Quality:

As publishers, we strive to produce every book to the
highest commercial standards.

The book has been carefully designed to minimise awkward
page turns and to make playing from it a real pleasure.

Particular care has been given to specifying acid-free, neutral-sized paper made
from pulps which have not been elemental chlorine bleached.

This pulp is from farmed sustainable forests
and was produced with special regard for the environment.

Throughout, the printing and binding have been planned to ensure a sturdy,
attractive publication which should give years of enjoyment.

If your copy fails to meet our high standards,
please inform us and we will gladly replace it.

Prayer

Words & Music by Rolf Lovland & Fionnuala Sherry

Dell'Amore Non Si Sa

Words & Music by Mauro Malavasi, Leonardo De Bernardini & Andrea Sandri

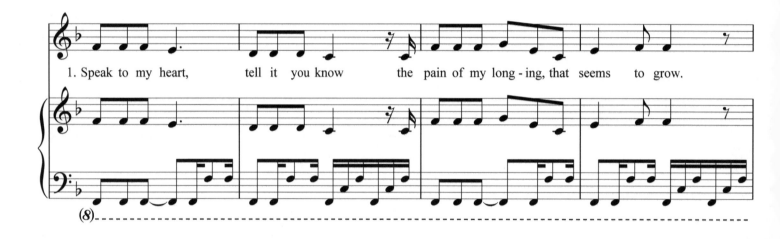

1. Speak to my heart, tell it you know the pain of my long-ing, that seems to grow.

Speak, oh, my star and tell me if he will come.

star - bright friend, please tell me if he will____ stay.____ }
who tells me al - ways on - ly the____ truth.____ }

Dell'- a - mo - re non si sa,____ quan-do

vien - e o se ne va.____ Dell'- a - mo - re non si sa,____

1.

quan-do sa - rà da do - ve ar - ri - ve-

14

Never Saw Blue

Words & Music by Mark Luna, Jeff Franzel & Tom Kimmel

18

Ave Maria

Music by Giulio Caccini

19

What You Never Know (Won't Hurt You)

Words & Music by Stephan Moccio & Hayley Westenra

I'm fall-ing___ for you.___ I'm fall-ing___ for you.___ My heart's torn___ in two.___ I'm fall-ing___ for you.___ What you nev-er know___ won't hurt___ you.___

24

26

Quanta Qualia

Composed and arranged by Patrick Hawes
Words by Andrew Hawes

Both Sides Now

Words & Music by Joni Mitchell

1. Rows and flows of an-gel hair___ and ice-cream cas-tles in the air.___ And
2. Moons and Junes and Fer-ris wheels.__ The diz-zy danc-ing way you feel___ as

fea-ther can-yons___ ev-'ry-where.__ I've looked at clouds that way.
ev-'ry fai-ry - tail comes real.__ I've looked at love that way.

Now they on-ly block the sun,___ they rain and snow___ on ev-'ry-one.___ So
Now it's just a - no-ther show, you leave 'em laugh-ing when you go.___ And

ma-ny things I would have done___ but clouds got in my way.
if you care don't let them know,___ don't give your-self a - way.

I've looked at clouds from both sides now,___ from up and down___ and
I've looked at love from both sides now,___ from give and take___ and
I've looked at life from both sides now,___ from win and lose___ and

To Coda

still___ some - how___ it's_____ cloud il - lu - sions I re - call. I real - ly___ don't know
still___ some - how___ it's_____ love's il - lu - sions I re - call I real - ly___ don't know
still___ some - how___ it's_____ life's il - lu - sions I re - call I real - ly___ don't know

May It Be
(from the film "The Lord Of The Rings")

Words & Music by Roma Ryan, Nicky Ryan & Eithne Ni Bhraonain

Bachianas Brasileiras No.5 Aria (Cantilena)

Composed by Heitor Villa-Lobos

Bridal Ballad
(from the film "The Merchant Of Venice")

Words by Edgar Allan Poe
Music by Jocelyn Pook

Con pedale

Verse 3:
And thus the words were spoken,
And this the plighted vow,
And, though my faith be broken,
And, though my heart be broken,
Here is a ring, as token
That I am happy now!

Verse 4:
Would God I could awaken!
For dream I know not how!
And my soul is sorely shaken
Lest an evil step be taken,
Lest the dead who is forsaken
May not be happy now.

The Mists Of Islay

Words & Music by Gavin Creed, Wishart Campbell & John McDonald

Lost on the mists of Is - lay.

O Mio Babbino Caro

Words by Giuseppe Adami
Music by Giacomo Puccini

si, ci vog-lio_an-da - re e se l'am-as-si_in-dar - no an-

-drei sui Pon - te Vec - chio ma per but-tar-mi_in Ar - no! Mi

strug-go_e mi tor - men - to! I Di - o,_____

vor - rei mor - rir!

Bab - bo, pie - ta, pie - ta!

Bab - ba, pie - ta, pie - ta!

50

Laudate Dominum

Composed by Wolfgang Amadeus Mozart

lau - da - - - te___ e - um, om - -

nes, om - - - nes po - - pu li.

Quo - niam con - fir - ma - ta est su - - per___

nos mi - se - re - cor - dia

53

et spi - ri - tu - i Saue - to. Si - - cut

e - - rat in prin - ci - - pi - o,

et nunc et sem - per, et in

sae - cu - la sae - - cu - -

55

Wiegenlied

Words & Music by Bernhard Flies & Friedrich Gotter

1. Schla - fe, mein Prinz - chen, schlaf ein! Es ruhn
2. Al - les un Schlos - se schon liegt,
3. Wer ist be - glückt - er als du?

nun Schäf - chen und Vö - ge - lein._____ Gart - en und Wie - se ver -
al - les in Schlum - mer ge - wiegt;_____ re - get kein Mäus - chen sich
Nichts als Ver - gnü - gen und Ruh!_____ Spiel - werk und Zuck - er voll -

- stummt,_____ auch micht ein Bien - chen mehr summt._____
mehr,_____ Kel - ler und Kü - che sind leer._____
- auf,_____ und noch ka - ros - sen im Lauf.

Lu - na mit sil - ber - nem Schein_____ gu - cket zum Fen - ster her -
Nur in der Zo - fe Ge - mach_____ tö - net ein Schmacht-en - des
Al - les be - sorgt und be - reit,_____ daß nur mein Prinz - chen nicht

- ein,_____ schla - fe beim sil - ber - nem schein._____
Ach!_____ Was für ein Ach mag dies sein?_____
schreit._____ Was wird da künf - tig erst sein?_____

Schla - fe, mein Prinz - chen, schlaf ein, schlaf ein,_____ schlaf ein!_____ Schlaf

1, 2.
ein,_____ schlaf ein!_____

3.
rit.
ein,_____ schlaf ein!

She Moves Through The Fair

Words by Padraic Colum
Traditional Music

moved through the fair.

Dido's Lament

Words by Nahum Tate
Music by Henry Purcell

When I am laid,___ am laid___ in earth, may my wrongs___ cre - ate___ no trou - ble, no trou - ble in___ thy breast. Re - -mem - ber me. Re - mem - ber me. But

ah!_____ For-get my fate. Re - mem - ber me. But

ah!_____ For - get my___ fate. Re - mem - ber me.

Re - mem - ber me. But ah!_____ For - get my

fate. Re - mem - ber me. But ah!_____ For - get my___

Forget my fate.